BATTLEFIELDS OF HONOR

Photographs by
MARK ELSON

Text by
JEANNINE STEIN

Foreword by
JAMES LIGHTHIZER

BATTLEFIELDS OF HONOR
AMERICAN CIVIL WAR REENACTORS

MERRELL
LONDON · NEW YORK

Two men portraying Union
reporters for *Harper's Weekly*
cover a battle in South
Mountain, Maryland.
Wet-plate photograph

FOREWORD

In 1865, as America's Civil War entered its fourth bloody, intolerable, and horrific year, Albert Champlain, a private in the 150th Ohio Volunteer Infantry, put pen to paper and attempted to make sense of the carnage and suffering. In doing so, he summarized the hopes of many across the contested land:

> *May an Overulling [sic] Providence continue to cause good to come out of evil, justice to be done to all men where injustice has long prevailed, and finally, peace, quiet, and harmony to come out of this terrible confrontation and our country's fiery ordeal.*

As we commemorate the 150th anniversary of this momentous occasion in American history, it seems only fitting that we too should take Private Champlain's words to heart and find new ways to cause some good to come from the fiery ordeal of the Civil War.

In *Battlefields of Honor: American Civil War Reenactors*, we are introduced to both Americans and non-Americans who are doing just that. From Pennsylvania to Georgia and beyond, these living historians are keeping this important history alive, and are sowing the seeds of history within the next generation—a most fitting and proper way to commemorate the Civil War.

In the work that follows, we also learn the "who," "what," "when," "where," "how," and, most importantly, "why" of what these men and women do to keep this history fresh in our collective consciousness. From the perspective of a lifelong preservationist, I am indebted to the work of my friends in the living-history community who bring color and life to the now-deathless fields that my organization, the Civil War Trust, has fought so hard to save.

With fresh and illuminating photography and insightful and engaging text, the team of Mark Elson and Jeannine Stein have done their subject justice, revealing the unique way in which people from all walks of life have chosen to honor and remember such a pivotal moment in the history of the United States.

James Lighthizer
President, Civil War Trust
Washington, D.C.

INTRODUCTION

The Camera is the eye of history
Mathew Brady

On a Civil War battlefield in Virginia, Confederate soldier Brandon Booth rises from under his wool blanket, brushes off the morning chill, and begins to make his breakfast. The year is not 1865 but 2012, and just hours ago Booth was battling twenty-first-century rush-hour traffic. This, then, is the life of modern Civil War reenactors—men, women, and children who recreate battles, camp life, and the day-to-day activities of Civil War soldiers and civilians.

Booth is one of thousands of people across the United States and further afield who feel an intense and personal connection to this historical period, and straddle two worlds many years apart. For them, reading about the war is not enough; they must immerse themselves in it via staged and free-form reenactments. Several days a year, they leave their jobs and homes to become battle-weary soldiers, courageous generals, dedicated nurses, and eager newspaper reporters, adopting not only the clothes of the era but also the language, mannerisms, food, and even the toiletries.

Reenacting the Civil War is more than an excuse for grown-ups with a penchant for history to play dress up. This cultural phenomenon has roots that go back to the war itself, when reenactments were used to recruit soldiers.

Reenactments vary in scope and flavor, from an abbreviated clash on a high-school football field to elaborately choreographed combat on the actual site of a Civil War battle. Reenactors, too, embrace various levels of authenticity. Some are content to march in imported polyester-blend uniforms and spend the night in a motor home. Others, called "authentics" or "hardcores," pay excruciating attention to detail, making sure the stitch counts in their uniforms are identical to those of period uniforms and sleeping on the ground, enduring the same hardships the soldiers

In this wet-plate photograph by Mark Elson, reenactor Guy William Gane III, portraying a Union officer, stands in front of the headquarters of Union general George G. Meade at Gettysburg National Military Park in Pennsylvania.

RIGHT

In the early morning, before the battle begins, reenactor Brandon Booth prepares a simple breakfast of ham, potatoes, and coffee. Booth is portraying a Confederate from the Second Mississippi Infantry at the 150th anniversary of the First Battle of Bull Run/ Manassas in Virginia.

lived through, including hypothermia, insect bites, and having little to eat.

Larger reenactments often feature other elements of wartime life, such as army camps and cavalry units, as well as living-history areas, which might include medical tents, members of the American Anti-Slavery Society, pubs, politicians' tents, and gambling dens. Entire families become involved, embracing every aspect of nineteenth-century life.

While most reenactments are put on for an audience, some private events, called "immersions," are for reenactors only. Such events—usually held in rugged, natural areas—are a chance for the participants to become completely engrossed in the life of a Civil War soldier. Although they will never know what that soldier truly experienced, this is probably the closest they will ever come.

Immersions can last for a week, with drills and arduous campaign-style marches. Rations are limited to what a Civil War soldier would have received, and all features of life at the time are recreated, including the vocabulary, the manners, and martial law. During unscripted battles, called "tacticals," no one knows the exact moves of the enemy or the end point, making skirmishes more realistic and exhilarating. Tacticals may not be as flamboyant as larger battles, but they are less about the performance and more about the adventure.

If reenactors surrender to the illusion willingly, they do so for different reasons. For some, recreating battles and events from a war fought 150 years ago is a way of reconnecting with a monumental period of America's past. As they stand on the same battlefield as the one on which soldiers fought a century and a half ago, the war

Janet Whaley, a human resources executive, finds a connection to the Civil War through her great-great-grandfather, Union soldier Elias Whaley. Here, she portrays a member of the United States Sanitary Commission in Redlands, California.

takes on a far greater meaning, one that reaches beyond history books. At a reenactment, the past is tangible, immediate, felt in the deafening thunder of cannon fire or the adrenaline rush of a cavalry charge.

Terry Handy, a teacher from California, has been reenacting since the 1970s, when going to events was something fun he would do with friends. But when he started researching the war in depth, reading book after book, the era began to come alive for him: "What got me excited was reading the accounts of the common soldier—what their life was like. I enjoyed the personal accounts, the stories from the soldiers themselves about what they ate and the sadness they felt."

That flipped a switch for Handy. He decided to honor those soldiers by exploring the hobby more seriously, recreating their life more realistically. His interest in reenacting has taken him to events across

the United States, from immersions in Louisiana to large public reenactments in Virginia.

Those reenactors whose ancestors were involved in the war participate to keep the memory of their predecessors alive and to honor their service. Many make an effort to appreciate the adversity their ancestors faced and the courage they displayed.

Janet Whaley's great-great-grandfather fought in the war, and the human resources manager from Southern California remembers him when she portrays a member of the United States Sanitary Commission, which lent aid to sick and injured soldiers and was a forerunner of the American Red Cross. "I think of what it must have been like for him coming off the battlefield," she says, "tired, possibly wounded in some way. What he must have felt, what it must have been like—is it still worth

fighting for this cause? I think I'm honoring his memory by trying to do it as accurately as possible, and by understanding some of the hardships he must have gone through."

Americans who reenact strive to display their patriotism. Some are literally born into it, as several generations of one family may embrace the hobby. Others find that the virtual time travel of a reenactment allows them temporarily to abandon such modern conveniences and nuisances as mobile telephones and traffic jams—not an easy thing to do.

"When I put on my uniform on Friday night," says Booth, a sales manager from Maryland, "I enter 1861. All I'm worried about the rest of the weekend is surviving and finding a good place to camp. I forget the modern world. I hate to come back. As exhausted as I get, I hate it. It's a jarring transition."

Reenactments also promise camaraderie and the thrill of fighting for a cause with strong alliances and few moral ambiguities. Still, it is not unusual to find reenactors who enjoy portraying both Union and Confederate soldiers, occasionally within the same reenactment. Sometimes it is done for the experience, and at other times to make troop sizes more even so that battles look more genuine.

Battles are the reenactments' centerpieces. They can be meticulously choreographed recreations of actual engagements, or far less structured and composed. At large public events, battles are often grand spectacles carried out with great fanfare and pageantry, taking place two or three times a day. Drummers and buglers accompany foot soldiers and cavalry troops as they assemble on the battlefield, flags waving. When combat begins, musket and cannon

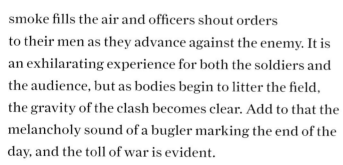

smoke fills the air and officers shout orders
to their men as they advance against the enemy. It is
an exhilarating experience for both the soldiers and
the audience, but as bodies begin to litter the field,
the gravity of the clash becomes clear. Add to that the
melancholy sound of a bugler marking the end of the
day, and the toll of war is evident.

When Guy William Gane III, an actor and model
from Buffalo, New York, began reenacting in the 1990s,
his adventures in battle were quite visceral: "When
I first started reenacting as a private, I felt a serious
weight on my chest before the battles. I had read
so much up to that point, that it was easy for me to
imagine bullets whizzing and cannon booming. I built
it up to make it feel like I was about to face a loaded
gun from thousands of men. It was great." As a
reenactor who takes on several different military
roles, he considers himself a living representative of
the Civil War: "I'm a guardian of the true history. I feel
like we were all here before, and perhaps we're back to
ensure the memories are not forgotten."

Most reenactments take place in the United States,
but it is not the only country in which men and women
recreate the Civil War. Reenactment communities
thrive in the United Kingdom, Australia, France,
Germany, and Sweden. At first, it may not make sense
to say that the war strikes a chord with them too, but
consider this: a large percentage of Civil War soldiers
were new European immigrants, and these modern-
day reenactors could well be their distant relatives.
Even if that is not the case, many European reenactors
connect with the lifestyle, romance, and mores of the
nineteenth century, which still live in the architecture,
entertainment, and literature of their homelands.

British reenactments, which attract people from various points across Europe, are often carried out with great enthusiasm on the sweeping grounds of impressive manor houses. Great attention is paid to detail, and reenactors stage battles with pomp and ceremony and fight them with much vigor. They often incorporate their own rituals, too, such as finishing the battle in time for afternoon tea. Such routines may not be authentic, but they lend the event a distinctive and appealing quality.

In the United States, reenacting is not limited to the mid-Atlantic and the South, although those areas are the hub of reenactment activity. Reenactments take place across the country, and physical relics of the war remain in unlikely places. Tucked away in Wilmington, California, a quiet, middle-class neighborhood about 30 miles (48 kilometers) to the

south of Los Angeles, is the Drum Barracks Civil War Museum, what remains of an expansive Union Army headquarters. Troops stationed at the barracks protected a great deal of the Southwest during the war, and ensured that California stayed in the Union. Both married and single officers were based there, and while husbands went off on patrols, their wives steadfastly waited for their return.

Women are integral to the staging of a reenactment, too. Although men may dominate the battlefield, women portray a variety of roles. Some tend camp while the men are off fighting, spending their time preparing and cooking food and tidying up. Others take on the roles of aid-givers, Southern belles, nurses and doctors, or craftswomen. At larger reenactments it is common to see women portraying such notable Civil War figures as Harriet Tubman, the

abolitionist; Clara Barton, a nurse who later founded
the American Red Cross; and Dr. Mary Edwards
Walker, a surgeon during the war and the only woman
ever to have received the Medal of Honor. Women
whose husbands portray such famous military and
political figures as Ulysses S. Grant and Jefferson
Davis often reenact their high-profile wives.

Some women, however, are not content to sit on
the sidelines during a battle. They would rather don a
uniform, tuck their hair under a cap, take up a musket,
and fight alongside the men, as some women actually
did during the war. Not all regiments accept female
soldiers, and many women work hard at gaining
acceptance, slogging through mud and carrying a
heavy knapsack just as the men do.

Paula Agar, a librarian at the University of York in
England, found she was not happy watching from afar
while her husband had all the fun on the battlefield:
"All the guys would come back off the field, talking
about the battle, and I felt left out. As soon as I put
the uniform on, I had so much more fun. During the
drills—I had never held a gun before in my life—I felt
more involved."

Whatever roles men and women choose, recreating
this lost era takes time, patience, and money, and an
entire industry has grown up around reenactments.
Some artisans and manufacturers who supply clothes
and accoutrements to reenactors spend hundreds of
hours making uniforms, hoop skirts, weapons, tents,
cooking pots, grain sacks, and everything else needed
to transform modern men and women into Civil War
soldiers and civilians.

In the 1960s, when reenactments in the United
States first became popular, reenactors had to cobble

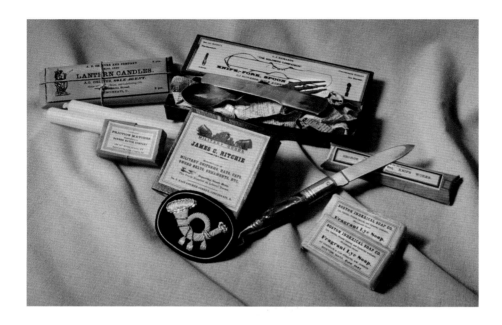

Owning authentic-looking accoutrements can deepen the experience for a reenactor. Sutler of Fort Scott, a Kansas-based store owned by Steve and Laura Dunfee, not only offers such personal items as clothing, military badges, eating utensils, and soap, but also sells them in packaging that is true to the period.

together clothes and supplies, which were often of questionable authenticity. Today, the most exacting artisans pay strict attention to the smallest of details, finishing buttonholes in the manner of the period, or creating genuine-looking packaging. In addition to selling their wares online, many set up shop at reenactments on Sutlers' Row (a sutler was a merchant who sold provisions to armies), offering both reproduction and authentic goods to reenactors and spectators alike. Some reenactors make their own clothes, following existing patterns or creating their own, even stitching them on antique treadle sewing machines.

Spending large sums of money pursuing their passion is not unusual for some reenactors. As they delve further into the hobby and the history of the war, they might trade their polyester-blend uniforms for hand-dyed woolens. When they do, they discover such companies as Kansas-based Sutler of Fort Scott, which sells museum-quality reproductions. The business grew out of co-owner Steve Dunfee's love of reenacting and collecting, and among the items he offers for sale are toothbrushes, writing pens, sewing-thread cards, and wallets, some of which he also manufactures. Owning smaller, personal items, he believes, is a way of capturing a soldier's essence, beyond weapons and uniforms. "It was the smallest, simplest comfort to have these items with them in the field," he explains, a remembrance of home.

Dunfee takes things one step further, packaging the items in boxes with labels that are either copies of originals or his own designs featuring period typefaces and graphics he has gone to great lengths to research. Although it is sometimes a painstaking process, for

A line of Union soldiers fires on Confederate troops at the 150th anniversary of the Battle of Wilson's Creek in Missouri.

the reenactor there is a payoff. "The more distractions you can take away," says Dunfee, "the better the experience and the more meaningful the education."

If all of this is about creating an illusion, it is a fairly impressive one. Taking part in a reenactment, or simply observing one, can be a transformational experience that just begins with the clothing. Reenactors often speak of losing their sense of time and place in the heat of battle, as troop lines advance and musket smoke fills the air.

For both reenactors and spectators, there are moments when the twenty-first century loosens its grip and the nineteenth takes over. Reenactors sense the modern world fading away when facing the enemy in trench warfare or when feeling the thunder of cannon fire in their bones. For spectators, watching the spectacle of hundreds of soldiers marching on the field accompanied by a fife-and-drum corps is an unparalleled event. But transcendent moments can be small in scale, too: waiting silently in the woods while the enemy approaches, or seeing women dressed in humble calico dresses tending to food in a cast-iron pot. "You lose the twenty-first century, looking over the line of soldiers coming off the hill, and in the battle, in the smoke and the confusion that happens," says Kevin Myers, who portrays an officer in Pridgeon's Shenandoah Legion in the mid-Atlantic.

To capture such moments for this book, photographer Mark Elson used a combination of 35-mm and wet-plate photography. The latter is a nineteenth-century photographic process that can be used to produce a negative image on a glass plate or a positive but reversed image on a metal plate, also known as a "tintype."

The popularity of reenacting the American Civil War is not limited to the United States; events are also staged in Europe and Australia. This reenactment took place on the grounds of Stanford Hall in Leicestershire, England.

Wet-plate photography was used during the Civil War by such early documentary photographers as Mathew Brady, Timothy O'Sullivan, and Alexander Gardner. The process is enjoying something of a renaissance, as photographers discover that, although challenging, it produces dreamy, vintage-looking images that no amount of sepia toning or digital manipulation can recreate.

The same methods and chemistry as those used 150 years ago are still employed today, but with a few tweaks. Some photographers use wooden sliding box or bellows cameras that have been handmade by modern-day craftspeople from period drawings and diagrams, while others also use refurbished nineteenth-century cameras. Most use lenses from the period, since reproducing them exactly is difficult. The glass lenses were hand-ground and extremely

sharp, although they retained natural distortions. Portrait lenses in particular have a distinctly sharp center that falls off toward the edges, creating the swirls and a softness that are some of the hallmarks of wet-plate photography. The chemicals used are based on nineteenth-century formulas that have been modified by modern-day photographers.

To take a wet-plate photograph, the photographer must first of all cover the plate with a thin, even coating of collodion, a syrupy solution of pyroxylin in a mixture of alcohol and ether. The plate is then dipped in a silver bath to make it light-sensitive. While the plate is still wet (hence the term "wet plate"), it is placed in a plate holder, which fits securely into the back of the camera. The photographer then removes the "dark slide" from the plate holder and exposes the plate by temporarily removing the lens cap, allowing light into

Examples of reproduction wet-plate cameras and period lenses include a sliding box camera, left, modeled after a Mathew Brady camera and built in England by Ivan Rose. A bellows field camera, right, built by Clovis Davis in the United States, is typical of what photographers would have used in the field during the Civil War. The lenses date from 1860.

Equipment used to expose and develop wet-plate photographs includes, from left, a small plate holder, a drying rack, a larger plate holder, and a silver-bath tank for sensitizing plates.

the camera; light conditions determine how long the lens cap remains off. After exposure, the dark slide is replaced so that the plate holder can be removed and taken to a portable darkroom, where the plate is developed, a process that takes about 10 to 15 seconds. To stop the developer, water is poured over the plate, which then goes into a fixer bath. Finally, the plate is placed in water to remove the fixer. The whole process is both tricky—weather, light, dust, and temperature can all affect the outcome—and physically demanding. But for those inspired by Brady, O'Sullivan, and Gardner, capturing images at reenactments with the same equipment and processes they used offers a rare opportunity to experience photography as they did.

Many people are surprised that the wet-plate process is still being used in an age when digital photography is ubiquitous and much simpler.

However, for anyone engaged in the making of glass-plate negatives and tintypes, there is the satisfaction of creating images by hand, guided by experience and intuition, rather than relying on the decisions of an electronic device.

Wet-plate photographers often come away with a greater appreciation not only for what their nineteenth-century predecessors had to endure to get their images, but also for their talent for producing well-designed and functional cameras and equipment. Although a few documents exist outlining how they devised and built their creations, such documents and their photographs are their only legacy. Unfortunately, Mathew Brady is not around to lecture on the finer points of wet-plate photography.

Reenactors and artisans keep history alive by visiting the past: are you ready to go with them?

THE SECRET LIVES OF REENACTORS

No one becomes a reenactor as a lark; it takes considerable time, money, and dedication to portray a Civil War soldier or civilian. So why do people do it?

Many have ancestors who fought in the war, and reenacting allows them to celebrate their memory and service. Some reenactors are fortunate enough to have their ancestors' diaries, war records, and photographs, all of which contain fascinating details about the period, information the reenactors often incorporate into their portrayals.

For history enthusiasts, reenacting provides an immersion in the era and an experience that books cannot supply. It is not unusual to find reenactors huddled together, discussing the minutia of a battle or arguing the finer points of states' rights while going in and out of character.

Entire families reenact together, enabling family members to spend time with one another away from computers and television. Parents bring children into the hobby and children bring parents. Friendships spawned at reenactments have lasted decades, just as they did during and after the war.

For everyone who participates, reenacting provides an opportunity to escape from the stress, complexity, and responsibilities of twenty-first-century life—if only for a little while.

PAGE 20
A Union reenactor stands guard in South Mountain, Maryland. The muskets behind him have been "stacked."
Wet-plate photograph

OPPOSITE
At the Drum Barracks Civil War Museum in Wilmington, California, a man portraying a journalist from the *Savannah Morning Dispatch* describes a scene to inspire the Confederate home front. During the war, some journalists also operated as spies.
Wet-plate photograph

This man, who has taken on the role of a civilian, forgoes wearing a traditional waistcoat in order to accommodate the hot weather.
Wet-plate photograph

A reenactor portraying a Union soldier holds a photograph of a loved one.
Wet-plate photograph

An interest in history drives Scot Buffington's fascination with the Civil War. As a reenactor, he is not content portraying only one role: opposite, pictured with his wife, Sarah, he is a farmer; below, standing in an orchard in New Market Battlefield State Historical Park, Virginia, he is a Union soldier heading off to war.

A group of men from Michigan portray Company B of the 102nd United States Colored Troop (USCT) at the Civil War Muster in Jackson, Michigan. The 102nd USCT has a particular significance for these men: formed in 1863, the regiment drew recruits from the Detroit area. By portraying part of the regiment, the reenactors are helping to keep alive the memory of the more than 180,000 black Union soldiers who fought in the war.

Scott Iwasaki, portraying a private in the Twentieth Maine Volunteer Infantry Regiment, attends a reenactment in Vista, California, with his three sons. The catalyst for the family becoming involved in reenactments was Scott's oldest son, Kyle, far right, and his interest in history.

Merritt Booth takes on the role of a banjo player and Confederate soldier in the Thirty-Seventh Virginia Infantry at a reenactment in Spotsylvania, Virginia. Booth, a sound engineer, often attends reenactments with his father, Brandon (also a Confederate soldier; see page 10), and enjoys the camaraderie and escape from modern-day life.

On a chilly morning on the McDowell Battlefield in Virginia, members of the Thirty-Seventh Virginia prepare breakfast around an open fire.

Choosing the role of a journalist allows reenactors to experience battles in a different way: they are given not only a bird's-eye view of the action but also access to the president, high-ranking officials, and common soldiers. Some who portray journalists also write about the reenactments they attend in the form of online news stories written in the vernacular of the day. Andrew Gage, posing with his wife, Michelle, reenacts Union journalist Nathaniel F. Ethell in Hartford City, Indiana.

Not all reenactors feel compelled to portray soldiers as heroes. This man at a reenactment in Moorpark, California, wanted to experience being a petty thief. During the Civil War, soldiers caught stealing were forced to wear a sign proclaiming their crime and then marched around camp.

This young man at Perryville Battlefield State Historic Site in Kentucky portrays a cavalry soldier in the Confederate Army of Tennessee. The army was active in the Western Theater, which included the states of Mississippi, Kentucky, Tennessee, and Georgia.

Cutting a dashing figure, Robert G. MacMillan portrays Major General James Ewell Brown "Jeb" Stuart of the Confederate Army of Northern Virginia at a reenactment in Moorpark.

Some reenactors feel an affinity with the foreigners who fought in the war. This man in South Mountain, Maryland, has taken on the role of an Irishman who joined the Fifty-Sixth Pennsylvania Volunteer Infantry. He has even perfected an Irish accent to make his portrayal more realistic.

Looking like a famous historical figure can be a good reason to reenact them; Fritz Klein, pictured in Hartford City, bears a striking resemblance to President Abraham Lincoln. A resident of Springfield, Illinois—Lincoln's hometown before the war— Klein has portrayed the former president for many years.

At a reenactment at McDowell Battlefield in Virginia, a reenactor portrays Confederate general Thomas Jonathan "Stonewall" Jackson down to the last detail, even holding a lemon, something Jackson was known to eat during battles. His horse also adds to the authenticity—by bearing a resemblance to the general's mount, Little Sorrell.

A reenactor in Moorpark, California, assumes the role of a Union private.

A man portrays a Confederate soldier in Winchester, Virginia. Black Confederate soldiers did exist during the war, but were not common.

Standing on a hill in New Market Battlefield State Historical Park, Virginia, a Union cavalry flag behind him, Dale Harrison assumes the role of Major General George Armstrong Custer, a cavalry officer during the Civil War.

Chuck Eberle, a descendant of Confederate general Robert E. Lee, portrays his ancestor at a reenactment of the Battle of Spotsylvania Court House in Virginia.

At a reenactment of the Battle
of Spotsylvania Court House, this
barefoot Confederate private's
mismatched uniform—part
civilian, part military—reveals
how troops had to go without
basic supplies toward the end
of the war.

A Union captain poses with his
sergeant and two privates in front
of the headquarters of Union
general George G. Meade at
Gettysburg National Military
Park in Pennsylvania.
Wet-plate photograph

A Union chaplain at a reenactment of the Battle of New Market administers comfort and spiritual guidance to soldiers, much like chaplains did during the war.

Reverend Alan Farley, a modern-day preacher, brings some realism to his portrayal of a Confederate preacher at a reenactment of the Battle of Spotsylvania Court House. Around the time of the battle, fought in 1864, a religious revival swept the Confederate Army of Northern Virginia.

A Confederate provost marshal patrols the camp at a reenactment in Leicestershire, England, keeping an eye out for stragglers and deserters.

OPPOSITE
A man portraying a Union soldier
stands guard at a camp in Acton,
California. In 1863, African
Americans were allowed to form
their own segregated regiments
commanded by white officers.
Wet-plate photograph

A Union cavalry trooper enjoys a
cigar in Central Coast, California.
Wet-plate photograph

Todd Beamis portrays a scruffy
Confederate infantryman at the
Drum Barracks Civil War Museum
in Wilmington, California.
Wet-plate photograph

Wearing a mourning outfit complete with veil, a woman pays tribute to fallen soldiers at a Veterans Day memorial service in San Gabriel, California.
Wet-plate photograph

Susan Ogle, director of the Drum
Barracks Civil War Museum, takes
part in reenactments to raise
awareness of Civil War history
and site preservation.
Wet-plate photograph

Reenactors portraying members of the Missouri State Guard, a legal militia formed at the start of the war to protect the state, display their flag at the 150th anniversary of the Battle of Wilson's Creek in Missouri.

Andrew Bowman, right, portrays
Andrew Jackson Smith in
Hartford City, Indiana. Smith,
a color sergeant and Medal of
Honor winner, was Bowman's
grandfather. Khabir Shareef,
center, takes on the role of
Martin Delany, the first African
American field officer in the
Union Army. Sam Meadows,
left, portrays a drummer.

REENACTORS ABROAD

The lure of the American Civil War extends far beyond US borders. Reenacting the war is immensely popular in Europe, where reenactments are held regularly throughout the spring and summer.

Many foreign reenactors are aware of the fact that some of their forebearers took part in the war as recent immigrants to the United States; some even portray their ancestors. For others, the appeal lies in connecting with this romantic, albeit bloody, part of American history. Mid-nineteenth-century Americans were not unlike their contemporaries in Europe; customs, mores, and even clothes were quite similar.

In common with Civil War reenactors in America, those in Europe go to great lengths to ensure that their portrayals are accurate. Reenactments abroad, however, can take on a distinct flavor: languages spoken include French, German, and Swedish, and commands often have to be translated.

Although parts of England resemble Civil War battlefields in the mid-Atlantic and Southern regions of the United States, it can be startling to see a battle being fought on the grounds of an English country house. The reenactments featured in this section took place on the grounds of two such houses—Stanford Hall in Leicestershire and Sewerby Hall in Yorkshire—where hundreds of reenactors gathered from across Europe.

Thousands of miles away from where American soldiers fought, the connection to the Civil War is very much alive.

PAGE 48
Union reenactors use fallen trees as protection during a battle in the woods.

RIGHT
A civilian dressed in his walking clothes observes a battle.

Reenacting allows men and women to portray anyone, from a beggar to a three-star general. This English reenactor assumes the role of a well-heeled gentleman.

Members of the Iron Brigade, an infantry brigade of the Union Army, assemble for roll call on the grounds of Stanford Hall.

Yankees open fire as the Confederates defend a makeshift plantation in the shape of Sewerby Hall.

An English reenactor
portrays both a Union and
a Confederate soldier.

At a reenactment of the Battle of Gettysburg, four British reenactors portray famous commanders. From left, Lieutenant Colonel Arthur Fremantle, an observer from the British Army, is joined by Colonel Edward Porter Alexander, General Robert E. Lee, and Lieutenant General James Longstreet of the Confederates.

A group of Swedish reenactors—including one woman—portrays Union soldiers at an American reenactment in Jackson, Michigan.

An English reenactor assumes the role of a Confederate artillery officer.

At a Union camp, an English
reenactor portrays a cook
preparing meals for the soldiers.

An English Confederate soldier
poses with his wife against
a backdrop of tents.

Members of the Lazy Jacks Mess, a British living-history group, take a break in their camp.

A group of Confederate soldiers relax at Stanford Hall. Their clothing and postures are typical of the period.

Reenactors portraying Confederate soldiers and civilians enjoy a picnic by a lily pond after a reenactment at Stanford Hall. During the war, soldiers and their wives did their best to maintain some semblance of normal life by relaxing together in camp.

A reenactor from Scotland dons a field uniform in his portrayal of a Confederate colonel.

A Union non-commissioned
officer is portrayed by an
English reenactor.

A British man portraying a Union
private stands in front of an early
American flag.

Some reenactors portray more than one character. This English reenactor assumes the role of a nineteenth-century gentleman and a Confederate private.

The fatigue of battle weighs
heavily on a Union soldier during
an engagement at Stanford Hall.

Holding his musket proudly at his side, an Italian reenactor portrays a Confederate soldier.

Three French reenactors playing the parts of Confederate soldiers await orders during a reenactment.

Italian and English Confederates perform drills before a skirmish.

At a reenactment at Stanford Hall, a concerned Confederate sergeant watches over his troops before entering the fray.

Following close behind her husband, an English woman, far left, portrays a male member of the Iron Brigade.

At a reenactment at Stanford Hall, a Union battle line finds itself at risk of being overrun by Confederate forces.

Confederate troops made up
of reenactors from the United
Kingdom and Italy advance
under fire.

Smoke fills the air as a
Union cannon is fired during
a reenactment on the grounds
of Sewerby Hall.

In the aftermath of a battle at
Sewerby Hall, fallen Union and
Confederate soldiers lie scattered
on the ground.

Reenactors from the Lazy Jacks
Mess living-history group portray
Union soldiers. The group is
renowned for its authenticity.

Two English reenactors take on
the roles of Confederate privates.

A Confederate private steadies his
nerves during a break in fighting
at Stanford Hall.

An American portraying
a Confederate soldier, center,
is flanked by his English and
Irish companions.

British reenactors portray
members of the Irish Brigade.
This Union infantry unit,
which consisted mostly of Irish
Americans in regiments from
Massachusetts, New York, and
Pennsylvania, was noted for
its bravery.

An English reenactor portraying a Union officer shouts commands to his men as musket smoke drifts through the woods at Stanford Hall.

Confederate soldiers at Stanford Hall search out the enemy during a tactical, a free-form and unscripted type of reenactment.

Confederates, some portrayed
by French and Belgian reenactors,
charge Union lines.

A young Confederate soldier becomes a battlefield casualty during a tactical at Stanford Hall.

WOMEN REENACTORS

The diverse tasks and roles taken on by women during the Civil War can be seen in reenactments of all aspects of the conflict, from civilian camp life to bloody encounters on the battlefield.

Which characters the women choose to portray in a reenactment may depend on how active they wish their parts to be; some women quietly cook and tend camp, while others adopt such roles as members of the United States Sanitary Commission, which secured medicine for soldiers and looked after the sick and wounded.

Some choose to portray "Bloomers," followers of activist Amelia Bloomer, who promoted women's rights, temperance, and the wearing of loose pants (or "bloomers" as they came to be known) under a skirt because they were more comfortable and practical than the long dresses of the day.

During the war, women also served as laundresses, nurses, and spies. Reenacting more high-profile historical figures, such as abolitionist Harriet Tubman, takes some research, but these portrayals help to shed light on the important contributions made by women.

Female reenactors also disguise themselves as male soldiers, fighting alongside the men, as some did during the war. If the masquerade is successful, spectators may be completely unaware that women make up some of the ranks.

Reenacting may seem like a boys' club, but women are an essential part of the activity.

PAGE 80
At a reenactment in Jackson,
Michigan, a woman prepares
to cook for the camp using a
Dutch oven, a type of cast-iron
cooking pot.

Women at a reenactment in California's Central Coast portray members of the United States Sanitary Commission, which provided care for the sick and injured during the war. The commission was a forerunner of the American Red Cross.

Showing what home life was like during the Civil War, these women go about their daily rituals at a cabin at New Market Battlefield State Historical Park in Virginia.

In Hartford City, Indiana,
a woman portrays abolitionist
Harriet Tubman, complete with
military pistol.

Two women portray Union
soldiers at a reenactment in
Chino, California.

As shown here, far right, at a reenactment in Acton, California, women often accompanied troops as laundresses, cooks, or nurses. Sometimes, they were married to non-commissioned officers.
Wet-plate photograph

Sutler of Fort Scott sets up a tent at a reenactment at Wilson's Creek, Missouri, selling everything from matches to clothing.

A woman at a reenactment in Hartford City tends to a Dutch oven. Such cooking pots were commonly used throughout the war.

Carrying her medicine case, a woman portrays a Confederate doctor at New Market Battlefield State Historical Park.

Two women hand-sew a quilt as part of an immersion event at McDowell Battlefield in Virginia. Sewing was an everyday activity for women during the war.

Wearing a formal day dress, Susan Ogle stands in the courtyard of the Drum Barracks Civil War Museum in Wilmington, California. The barracks, which housed both married and single officers, were established in 1861 to secure California for the Union.

Wet-plate photograph

A woman dons the work clothes of a slave at a McDowell Battlefield reenactment. Confederate officers sometimes took male slaves with them to the war, to act as their servants, while female slaves typically stayed and worked on the plantations.

Wearing an outfit she made herself, reenactor Maegen Hensley poses in front of the Drum Barracks Civil War Museum. Hensley is a member of the Historical Citizens Association, a nonprofit Southern California reenacting group that seeks to educate the public about American history. *Wet-plate photograph*

A Confederate officer stands with
his wife and young servant on a
field at Perryville Battlefield State
Historic Site in Kentucky.

Officers' wives accompany Union
troops at New Market Battlefield
State Historical Park.

A woman portraying a male Union bugler stands behind an officer at McDowell Battlefield in Virginia.

At a reenactment in Moorpark, California, a woman portrays a Southerner in a Confederate camp. Troops stand at the ready in the background.

At the time of the war, some women began advocating for equal rights. Among them were Bloomers, here being portrayed at Perryville Battlefield State Historic Site. The women were followers of Amelia Bloomer, who, among other things, believed that women should wear pantaloons to afford them greater movement. The woman in the center holds a pamphlet promoting women's rights.

A group of Southern women,
wearing utilitarian work clothes
and aprons, provide food for
soldiers at McDowell Battlefield.

Two women honor the Civil War dead at the Confederate cemetery in Raymond, Mississippi.

Standing in front of a wood cabin on McDowell Battlefield, a young woman prepares to go about her day.

A woman portrays a shackled slave at a reenactment in Hartford City, Indiana. Some slaves continued to carry out their duties on plantations until the end of the war.

Lana Baily, another member
of the Historical Citizens
Association, proudly displays
her handmade winter outfit
at the Drum Barracks Civil War
Museum in California.
Wet-plate photograph

THE BATTLE

Reenactments revolve around the battle. Both reenactors and spectators live for a spirited North–South clash, complete with musket and cannon fire and thundering cavalry troops.

Battles can be meticulously choreographed, free-flowing and loose, or somewhere in between. Some include detailed maneuvers based on actual Civil War skirmishes, while others unfold with the barest of outlines. Either way, battles offer reenactors and spectators a taste of nineteenth-century warfare, a chance to see what soldiers and officers were up against: relentless fighting and chaos, and the threat of sustaining serious injuries or becoming a prisoner of war.

Battles are often awe-inspiring sights. Seeing hundreds of soldiers crest a hill, flags waving, is a breathtaking experience, one that newcomers do not readily forget. It is one thing to look at an illustration of a regimental band accompanying troops on a field, but quite another actually to hear the uplifting notes and feel the ground shake as the cavalry rides by.

Reenactors often talk about losing their sense of time and place during a battle, even when onlookers are only a short distance away. With their fellow troops all around them, their focus is squarely on facing down the enemy, listening to officers' commands, and always protecting their comrades-in-arms.

PAGE 98
A Confederate battle line moves in a snake-like formation toward Union troops at the New Market Battlefield State Historical Park in Virginia.

LEFT
Obscured by musket smoke, a Union battle line takes aim at advancing Confederate troops at the New Market Battlefield State Historical Park.

At a recreation of the Battle of Spotsylvania Court House in Virginia, a group of reenactors portrays Confederate pioneers, whose duties included clearing obstructions and building trenches for the troops.

In the aftermath of battle,
members of the First Texas
Volunteer Infantry gather for a
photograph. For soldiers away
from home for the first time,
posing for a photographer was
a significant experience.
Wet-plate photograph

ABOVE AND OPPOSITE, TOP
The Second Mississippi Infantry,
a Confederate regiment, lines
up for morning inspection at the
150th anniversary of the First
Battle of Bull Run/Manassas
in Virginia.

RIGHT
During the Civil War, bands
similar to this one, pictured at
a reenactment in Virginia, were
often used to raise soldiers'
morale as they went into battle.
The musicians also performed
at ceremonies and concerts.

2ᵈ MISS.

LEFT

A bugler with a Union militia unit stands with his instrument tucked under his arm at the 150th anniversary of the Battle of Wilson's Creek in Missouri. During the Civil War, drums and bugles were used to communicate battlefield orders to the troops, since the instruments could be heard above the din of the fighting.

One reenactor takes on two
different Confederate roles. Below,
center, he portrays a member of
the Second Mississippi Infantry in
1861 at the 150th anniversary of the
First Battle of Bull Run/Manassas.
Opposite, without a beard, he is
a soldier with the Thirty-Seventh
Virginia Infantry engaged in
trench warfare in 1864 at a
reenactment of the Battle of
Spotsylvania Court House.

Confederate soldiers' weapons and kits are stored in the trenches at a reenactment of the Battle of Spotsylvania Court House.

Standing third from the left, a reenactor portraying Union general Ulysses S. Grant gathers with his staff at a reenactment of the Battle of Spotsylvania Court House.

Members of the Fifth New York Volunteer Infantry convene at Moorpark, California. Led by Colonel Abram Duryée, the unit was also known as Duryée's Zouaves, after the soldiers' distinctive uniforms modeled on those of the French light infantry regiments known as Zouaves.

A reenactor at the Drum Barracks
Civil War Museum in Wilmington,
California, portrays Confederate
general George E. Pickett in full
battle uniform. Binoculars, here
being carried in their case, were
essential for directing the troops.
Wet-plate photograph

Two Union officers, wearing the
insignia of the Second Corps of
the Army of the Potomac, pose
with their weapons at a
reenactment in Acton, California.
Wet-plate photograph

Union soldiers from a New York
regiment stand with their weapons
and gear in Gettysburg National
Military Park, Pennsylvania,
before marching into battle.
Wet-plate photograph

Confederate troops at a reenactment of the Battle of Spotsylvania Court House march somberly past a cannon on the battlefield.

Union soldiers aim their muskets at Confederate troops during a clash at the McDowell Battlefield historical site in Virginia.

After a hard-fought battle, Confederate troops march through the hilly countryside of McDowell Battlefield.

His eyes fixed on advancing Confederate troops, this Union soldier waits behind earthworks at a reenactment of the Battle of Spotsylvania Court House.

A Confederate soldier acting as an early morning lookout surveys the battlefield from behind a trench wall, scouting for Union troops.

Under attack from Union artillery fire, Confederate troops take shelter at a reenactment of the Battle of Spotsylvania Court House.

Confederate soldiers in the trenches at a Battle of Spotsylvania Court House reenactment furiously load their weapons before taking on Union troops.

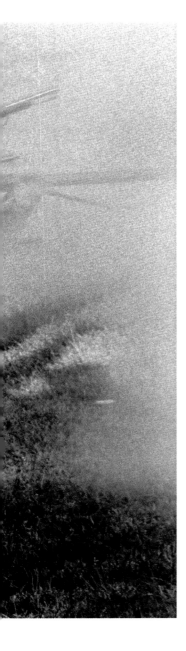

ABOVE
A close-range firefight
between Union and Confederate
troops takes place in Moorpark,
California.

LEFT
A Confederate battle line
unleashes a volley of bullets
at Union troops at a reenactment
in Hartford City, Indiana.

ABOVE AND OPPOSITE, TOP
Cavalry troops in San Diego,
California, charge the enemy.
Reenactors who choose to portray
cavalry troopers have the same
responsibilities as their Civil War
counterparts had, and must look
after the welfare of their horse.

Union soldiers advance up
a hillside toward Confederate
troops at a reenactment at
McDowell Battlefield, Virginia.

A Union Color Guard retreats
from the enemy during a
reenactment at the New Market
Battlefield State Historical Park
in Virginia. The Color Guard
is responsible for protecting the
flag during a battle.

ABOVE
At a reenactment in South
Mountain, Maryland, Confederate
soldiers of Cutshaw's Battery fire
a 12-pounder field howitzer.

LEFT
Smoke fills the air following
deafening cannon fire from Union
artillery at Moorpark, California.

With his field pack strapped to
his back and a pipe in his mouth,
a Union soldier is ready for a
long march.
Wet-plate photograph

A sunburned Union private
stands at attention after a battle
in South Mountain.
Wet-plate photograph

Four men portraying members of the Confederate First Virginia Volunteer Infantry in Southern California don uniforms typical of the early part of the war.
Wet-plate photograph

A Confederate cavalry sergeant
major shows off his revolver
and Henry repeating rifle at
a reenactment in California's
Central Coast.
Wet-plate photograph

Carrying his bedroll, haversack,
and musket, a reenactor at
Gettysburg National Military
Park, Pennsylvania, portrays a
Confederate soldier on the move
from one battle to the next.
Wet-plate photograph

A young Union soldier waits
for his marching orders at the
site of the Battle of Raymond
in Mississippi.

In preparation for a long march,
a Confederate private in Acton,
California, is loaded down with
his gear and weapon.
Wet-plate photograph

Confederate troops charge across rough, boulder-strewn terrain toward Union forces at the 150th anniversary of the Battle of Wilson's Creek in Missouri.

Confederate cavalry troops leave the battlefield victorious at the 150th anniversary of the Battle of Wilson's Creek.

On a cold morning at McDowell Battlefield, a blast of musket fire lights up the air as Confederate soldiers take on the Union Army.

A Union battle line displays its flag before facing Confederate troops at McDowell Battlefield in Virginia.

At the 150th anniversary of the Battle of Wilson's Creek, a Confederate officer dressed in an early Civil War uniform, right, prepares to enter the fray, sword in hand. On the opposite page, top, the same officer yells commands to his troops; moments later, they begin a withdrawal after coming under heavy attack from the Union Army.

RIGHT
With Union dead littering the field, Confederate troops fire at Union lines at the 150th anniversary of the First Battle of Bull Run/Manassas.

OPPOSITE, TOP, AND ABOVE
While Union troops hold the line
at the 150th anniversary of the
First Battle of Bull Run/Manassas
in Virginia, Confederates steadily
advance under fire.

Union privates stand in trenches
built especially for a reenactment
of the Battle of Spotsylvania
Court House.

Confederate troops attempt to hold off Union soldiers breaching the trenches at a Battle of Spotsylvania Court House reenactment.

A Union sergeant, center, endeavors to hold the line as Confederates rapidly approach his ranks at the New Market Battlefield State Historical Park in Virginia.

OPPOSITE
A Union journalist interviews
a corporal after a battle in South
Mountain, Maryland.
Wet-plate photograph

A Union officer, left, and private
in South Mountain stand in battle
dress, ready for war.
Wet-plate photograph

Wearing tartan trousers and a
distinctive hat, this Union soldier
in California's Central Coast is
easily identified as belonging
to the Seventy-Ninth New York
Highlanders, a regiment
comprised of Scots or those
of Scottish descent.
Wet-plate photograph

A woman at the Drum Barracks Civil War Museum in Wilmington, California, waits for her husband to return from battle. The barracks were home to married and single officers during the war. *Wet-plate photograph*

Portraying a private from the early part of the Civil War, this reenactor at the Drum Barracks Civil War Museum is equipped with a bayonet, canteen, musket, haversack, and bedroll.
Wet-plate photograph

A woman in mourning sits outside the Drum Barracks Civil War Museum. Women of the period would typically wear mourning clothes for at least a year after the death of a loved one.
Wet-plate photograph

The Color Guard of a Union
regiment gathers around its flag
in Moorpark, California. These
men are examples of "authentics,"
reenactors who pay great
attention to their appearance
and demeanor.
Wet-plate photograph

Confederate soldiers in South
Mountain, Maryland, display
company strength following
a battle.
Wet-plate photograph

BEHIND THE ILLUSION

If a Civil War reenactment requires an army of soldiers, the soldiers require an army of behind-the-scenes artisans, whose work lends an extra level of authenticity to the event.

At a reenactment, those craftspeople can be found on Sutler's Row, where they sell everything a nineteenth-century soldier or civilian could want: clothing, eating utensils, matches, furniture, guns, weaponry, cartridge belts, knapsacks, and blankets. As reenactors have increasingly demanded more genuine-looking reproductions to help them carry off their portrayals, so sutlers have answered the call.

Some recreate uniforms that are authentic to the last detail, using extensive knowledge of historical clothing and textiles to produce period-correct, museum-quality fabric and clothes. Often, reenactors who possess sewing and pattern-making skills produce their own clothes and accoutrements, consulting illustrations, drawings, photographs, and actual artifacts to ensure styles and features are correct.

Efforts to make reenactments as authentic as possible do not end there: musicians often play period music on antique or reproduction instruments, while cooks produce such food and drink as meat pies, ice cream, and sarsaparilla using only ingredients available at the time.

This may seem like an enormous amount of time and effort, but it is hardly wasted. Such dedication and attention to the tiniest of details help to create the remarkable moments, both grand and humble, that seamlessly transport reenactors and spectators to another time and place.

PAGE 138
The camp cook prepares some meat for a meal. The limited provisions for Civil War soldiers would have included meat, cornmeal, beans, and coffee. *Wet-plate photograph*

LEFT
At a reenactment of the Battle of Perryville at the Perryville Battlefield State Historic Site in Kentucky, Chad Greene portrays a Union colonel.

Confederate troops prepare to charge at a reenactment of the Battle of Perryville. The original battle was fought in 1862.

A Confederate soldier finds respite in a makeshift tent known as a "shebang" before going into battle at the 150th anniversary of the Battle of Wilson's Creek, Missouri. Among his food and cooking utensils arranged on the ground, below, is a single brass candlestick.

Robert Lee Hodge, a filmmaker and advocate of the preservation of Civil War battlefields, portrays a Union soldier at New Market Battlefield State Historical Park in Virginia.

A Union soldier poses with his musket and bayonet at Gettysburg National Military Park in Pennsylvania.
Wet-plate photograph

A Union soldier catches his first glimpse of the enemy during a tactical at Raymond Battlefield in Mississippi. He leaves the protection of a wooded area with a few of his fellow soldiers to advance across an open field. Shooting straight on and leaving himself vulnerable, he risks being killed—and is.

A Union soldier at the Drum Barracks Civil War Museum in Wilmington, California, poses with his equipment, which includes a cartridge belt, a book, a bayonet, a musket, a coffee cup and pot, a plate, a canteen, a knife and fork, and a small bag containing personal items. Below, with everything securely packed away, the same soldier stands in full marching order. Each piece of his equipment was produced by modern-day artisans, either by hand or using machines from the period.

Wet-plate photographs

In 1863, civilians under siege
during the Vicksburg Campaign
in Mississippi would sometimes
take refuge in dugouts they had
fashioned themselves in nearby
hillsides. To make these dirt-floor
dwellings as homelike and livable
as possible, the besieged civilians
furnished them with rugs and
furniture from their own homes.
Life went on, albeit with fewer
amenities. These reenactors
at a reenactment at Raymond
Battlefield lived in reproduction
dugouts during the event,
recreating various aspects of
dugout life. They slept, cooked,
ate, and entertained one another
as the battles raged around them.

LEFT
Reenactors take a break from the
fighting to enjoy an afternoon
dance at New Market Battlefield
State Historical Park.

Confederate soldiers from a North Carolina regiment prepare the midday meal at a camp in South Mountain, Maryland.
Wet-plate photograph

Dressed in the informal style of a
frontiersman, a sutler in California's
Central Coast carries a revolver and
knife for protection.
Wet-plate photograph

Sutlers in the Central Coast show
off their wares and temptations.
Wet-plate photograph

An immersion event in the mountains of Southern California recreates Camp Ford, a training camp for new Confederate recruits established in 1862 near Tyler in Texas. A civilian, top left, soon to be a soldier, helps set up the camp; later, top right, a seasoned veteran of the Confederate Army keeps new, unseen troops in line. These same troops, bottom right, take an oath of allegiance while being sworn in by the company captain. In another part of the camp, bottom left, a sutler displays canned fruits, lemonade, and cigars. Sutlers sold food and other necessities so soldiers could augment their meager allowances. Instead of cash, soldiers used stamps as payment.

RIGHT, TOP AND BOTTOM
At the same immersion event in Southern California, newly recruited soldiers about to leave their civilian lives behind fall into line, top, and enjoy their last taste of freedom at the sutler tent.

Wet-plate photographs

During the Civil War, the bodies of soldiers killed in action would often be embalmed within days. This reenactor portrays an embalming surgeon in the living-history civilian camp at Cedar Creek Battlefield in Virginia.

Civil War camps were sometimes visited by performers, who would entertain the troops between campaigns. This sword swallower at a reenactment in Hartford City, Indiana, was a major attraction.

Two reenactors portray members of a Confederate militia unit at the 150th anniversary of the Battle of Wilson's Creek, which took place close to the actual battlefield in Missouri. Both the Confederate and the Union army incorporated militia units during the first year of the Civil War.

RIGHT AND OPPOSITE, TOP
In the opening battles of the Civil War, regular army units fought alongside local militia groups, which had their own uniforms. Sometimes, both sides would be wearing similar clothing and colors, making it difficult to distinguish between them when gun smoke clouded the air. At the 150th anniversary of the First Battle of Bull Run/Manassas in Virginia, Confederate troops, right, face off against Union troops, opposite, all wearing red shirts.

RIGHT
At the 150th anniversary of the First Battle of Bull Run/ Manassas, officers inspect a line of hundreds of Confederate soldiers anxiously waiting for battle. The reenactment was staged near the actual battlefield in Virginia.

LEFT
Confederate cavalry troops
guard the flank at a reenactment at
the Perryville Battlefield State
Historic Site in Kentucky.

Confederate soldiers practice morning drills before a battle at McDowell Battlefield in Virginia.

Union soldiers line up for inspection at a reenactment at McDowell Battlefield. The building in the distance dates back to the Civil War.

Confederate reenactors head back to camp after an encounter with Union troops at Cedar Creek Battlefield.

At McDowell Battlefield, Union soldiers maneuver into position ahead of battle.

Confederate soldiers in South Mountain, Maryland, reload a cannon. This procedure, which consists of numerous steps, can take several minutes to complete.

Confederate troops line up for morning inspection at McDowell Battlefield. Supply issues often forced Confederate soldiers to piece together their uniforms, resulting in a wide variety of hats, coats, and pants.

Taking advantage of a break between drills, three Union soldiers at McDowell Battlefield relax next to a woodpile. Farmers often dreaded having soldiers camp on their land, since the men would take firewood and food.

As campfire smoke fills the early morning air, Union soldiers at McDowell Battlefield gather for breakfast at the mess tent. Reenactors pay close attention to all aspects of camp life, carrying their food in wooden crates, sleeping under canvas tents, and preparing their meals using period recipes.

At Raymond Battlefield in Mississippi, Union officers stand in front of their encampment in the woods. Part of the "authentic" experience is sleeping on the ground no matter what the weather, with only a sheet of canvas and a blanket for protection against the elements.

Confederate soldiers standing in a cottonfield on the Raymond Battlefield site in Mississippi carry a battle flag from 1863 that was often used by regiments from Missouri.

At Raymond Battlefield a man portrays a Confederate private of the Western Theater fighting in the Vicksburg Campaign of 1863.

At a reenactment in Jackson, Michigan, a man portrays a Confederate soldier recently captured by the Union Army. His tattered uniform is the result of hard campaigning.

At McDowell Battlefield, Union troops wait for an officer's command before heading into battle.

Union soldiers at McDowell Battlefield line up for inspection at their encampment in the woods.

Portraying President Abraham Lincoln requires special skills: one should not only look the part, but also be able to capture the man's down-to-earth persona. Don Ancell, pictured here at the Drum Barracks Civil War Museum in Wilmington, California, has been playing the part of Lincoln at reenactments and other events for more than fifteen years.

Wet-plate photograph

THEN AND NOW

Janet Whaley portrays a woman in mourning (see pages 44–45); above, she stands outside her office in Pasadena, California. The human resources executive also portrays a member of the United States Sanitary Commission (see page 11).

Paula and Greg Agar portray members of the Iron Brigade (see page 68). In real life, the English reenactors—pictured above at York railway station—both work at the University of York, Paula as a librarian, and Greg as a college porter.

Merritt Booth, top left, and
Brandon, his father, take on roles
as Confederate soldiers (see
pages 112 and 10, respectively).
Above, away from the battlefield,
Merritt, a sound engineer, and
Brandon, a sales manager, stand
outside their home in Maryland.

TIMELINE

1860

NOVEMBER 6

Abraham Lincoln is elected the sixteenth president of the United States.

DECEMBER 20

South Carolina becomes the first of eleven Southern states to secede from the Union.

DECEMBER–FEBRUARY 1861

Six more Southern states follow South Carolina's example and secede from the Union: Mississippi, Florida, Alabama, Georgia, Louisiana, and Texas.

1861

JANUARY 9

Star of the West, an unarmed merchant vessel trying to re-supply Fort Sumter in South Carolina, is fired on by Confederate artillery at the entrance to Charleston harbor and forced to turn back.

MARCH 4

Lincoln is inaugurated as president.

APRIL 12

Fort Sumter is fired on by Confederate forces. The Civil War begins.

APRIL 15

Lincoln calls for 75,000 volunteers to stop the insurrection in South Carolina. This action spurs yet more Southern states to secede from the Union. Between April 17 and May 20, Virginia, Arkansas, Tennessee, and North Carolina join the other seven breakaway states to form the Confederate States of America.

APRIL 19

Lincoln orders a naval blockade of all ports in the Confederacy. In Maryland, the Sixth Massachusetts Infantry is attacked by a secessionist mob while marching through Baltimore. Four soldiers and twelve civilians are killed.

APRIL 20

Colonel Robert E. Lee resigns his commission in the United States Army. By June, he has been made a Confederate general by Jefferson Davis, president of the Confederacy.

MAY 20

Richmond, Virginia, replaces Montgomery, Alabama, as the capital of the Confederacy.

MAY 24

Colonel Elmer E. Ellsworth of the Union Army is killed by an innkeeper in Alexandria, Virginia. The first officer to die in the war, he becomes a martyr for the North.

JULY 21

The First Battle of Bull Run (called the First Battle of Manassas in the South) is fought in Virginia. Confederate forces rout the Union Army in the first major battle of the war.

AUGUST 10

The Battle of Wilson's Creek is fought in Missouri. Union general Nathaniel Lyon is killed, and the Confederates score another victory on the heels of Bull Run/Manassas.

NOVEMBER 1

George B. McClellan is named general-in-chief of the Union Army.

NOVEMBER 8

The Union Navy seizes James A. Mason and John Slidell—Confederate commissioners to Great Britain and France, respectively—from the British steamer *Trent*. This act creates tension between the United States and Great Britain and raises the possibility of armed conflict.

NOVEMBER 19

Julia Ward Howe writes 'Battle Hymn of the Republic'.

1862

FEBRUARY 6

Confederate forces surrender Fort Henry, Tennessee, to Union general Ulysses S. Grant, thus placing the Cumberland and Tennessee rivers under Union control.

FEBRUARY 12–16

Fort Donelson, Tennessee, is captured by Union forces. This victory makes General Grant a household name.

FEBRUARY 23 – JUNE 9

The Shenandoah Valley Campaign is conducted in Virginia. Under Lieutenant General Thomas Jonathan "Stonewall" Jackson, Confederate troops win striking victories for the South.

MARCH 7–8

The Battle of Pea Ridge (called the Battle of Elkhorn Tavern in the South) is fought in northern Arkansas. The Union secures a hard-won victory against Confederate forces, which include three Native American regiments.

MARCH 9

Two ironclads, the USS *Monitor* and the CSS *Virginia*, fight in a battle near Hampton Roads, Virginia. Little damage is done to either vessel, but this first clash between armor-plated ships changes the face of naval warfare forever.

MARCH 28

The Battle of Glorieta Pass in New Mexico Territory results in a Union victory.

APRIL 6-7

The Battle of Shiloh is fought in Tennessee. Although the battle is considered a victory for the North, the fierce two-day fight results in almost 24,000 casualties.

APRIL 16

The Confederate states adopt conscription.

APRIL 25

New Orleans is captured by Union admiral David Farragut, thus closing the strategically valuable port to the Confederacy.

JUNE 25 – JULY 1

The Seven Days' battles—a series of six major battles, including Gaines's Mill on June 27 and Malvern Hill on July 1—are fought to the east of Richmond, Virginia. They result in thousands of casualties and the abandonment of the Peninsular Campaign by General McClellan. Continuing his rise as a commander in the Confederate forces, General Lee takes control of the Army of Northern Virginia.

AUGUST 29-30

The Second Battle of Bull Run (called the Second Battle of Manassas in the South) results in another Confederate victory near the same battleground as fought on the year before.

SEPTEMBER 17

The Battle of Antietam (called the Battle of Sharpsburg in the South) takes place in Maryland. With more than 23,000 casualties, this battle, a marginal victory for Union forces, is considered the single bloodiest day of the Civil War.

SEPTEMBER 22

Following the Union success at Antietam, President Lincoln issues the preliminary Emancipation Proclamation.

OCTOBER 8

The Battle of Perryville, Kentucky, results in a Union victory.

DECEMBER 13

The Battle of Fredericksburg is fought near the Rappahannock River in Virginia. Confederate forces under General Lee soundly defeat the Union Army of the Potomac, commanded by Major General Ambrose E. Burnside.

DECEMBER 31 – JANUARY 2, 1863

The Battle of Stones River (called the Battle of Murfreesboro in the South) is fought in Tennessee. Confederate troops are defeated in a decisive battle.

1863

JANUARY 1

Lincoln issues the Emancipation Proclamation, which declares that, with regard to the states of the Confederacy, "all persons held as slaves ... are, and henceforward shall be free."

JANUARY 1-22

The Army of the Potomac endures the "Mud March," an ill-fated troop movement along the Rappahannock River.

APRIL 2

In the Confederate capital of Richmond, Virginia, food shortages and high prices lead to bread riots.

MAY 1-4

The Battle of Chancellorsville, Virginia. Although the battle ends in a decisive victory for the South, General Jackson is badly wounded and dies seven days later.

JUNE 9

The Battle of Brandy Station, Virginia. The outcome of the battle, the largest cavalry engagement of the war, is inconclusive.

JUNE 20

West Virginia secedes from Virginia to become the thirty-fifth state in the Union.

JULY 1-3

The Battle of Gettysburg is fought in southern Pennsylvania. Considered the turning point of the war, this Union victory was the conflict's bloodiest battle, resulting in more than 51,000 casualties.

JULY 4

After several months of siege warfare, the Mississippi River stronghold of Vicksburg falls to Union forces, splitting the Confederacy in half.

JULY 13–16

Sparked by the Union draft, the New York City draft riots leave at least 105 people dead. Among the victims of the mob violence—at that time the worst riots in American history—are eleven black men, eight soldiers, and two policemen.

AUGUST 21

Lawrence, Kansas, is sacked by Quantrill's Raiders, a group of pro-Confederate guerrillas led by William Clarke Quantrill.

SEPTEMBER 19–20

The Battle of Chickamauga is fought in northwestern Georgia. One of the biggest battles of the war, with more than 34,000 casualties, it ends in a Confederate victory.

NOVEMBER 19

Lincoln delivers the Gettysburg Address at the dedication of the Soldiers' National Cemetery in Gettysburg, Pennsylvania. Fewer than 300 words long, and declaring that the nation "shall have a new birth of freedom," the speech is destined to become one of the greatest in American history.

NOVEMBER 23–25

The Battle of Chattanooga is fought among the hills of southern Tennessee. The decisive moment comes when Union troops capture a heavily fortified position on Missionary Ridge, routing the stunned Confederates.

1864

FEBRUARY 17

In South Carolina, the Confederate submarine CSS *Hunley* sinks the USS *Housatonic* at the entrance to Charleston harbor.

MARCH 9

General Grant is appointed lieutenant general, becoming the commander of all Union armies.

MARCH 10 – MAY 22

The Union's Red River Campaign, a series of battles along the Red River in Louisiana, takes place.

APRIL 12

The Battle of Fort Pillow, Tennessee, which ends in a victory for General Nathan Bedford Forrest and his Confederate troops. There are conflicting accounts of a massacre of both white and black Union soldiers.

MAY 5–7

The Battle of the Wilderness takes place near the Rapidan River, Virginia. Desperate fighting occurs amid thick woods, with little gained by either side except a total of almost 30,000 casualties. Wounded Union soldiers die in the resulting wildfire.

MAY 7

The Atlanta Campaign begins with Union general William T. Sherman advancing against Confederate general Joseph E. Johnston and his Army of Tennessee.

MAY 8–19

The Battle of Spotsylvania Court House, Virginia. A series of fierce engagements includes hand-to-hand combat. Once again, the casualties are staggering, with neither side gaining the upper hand.

MAY 11

Confederate cavalry commander Major General James Ewell Brown "Jeb" Stuart is killed at the Battle of Yellow Tavern, Virginia.

MAY 15

Confederate forces win the Battle of New Market, fought in the Shenandoah Valley, Virginia. The victorious side includes 257 cadets from the Virginia Military Institute.

JUNE 3

The Battle of Cold Harbor, Virginia. In this disastrous defeat for the North, approximately 7000 Union soldiers are killed or wounded within the first hour or so of fighting.

JUNE 10

The Battle of Brice's Cross Roads, Mississippi, is fought between the forces of General Forrest and those of Union commander Brigadier General Samuel D. Sturgis. In one of Forrest's finest victories, the Union Army is routed.

JUNE 19

While crowds watch from nearby cliffs, the USS *Kearsarge* sinks the feared commerce raider CSS *Alabama* off Cherbourg, France, where it was due to undergo a refit.

JUNE 27

As part of General Sherman's Atlanta Campaign, the Battle of Kennesaw Mountain is fought near Marietta, Georgia, resulting in a Confederate victory.

JULY 30

A mine in Petersburg, Virginia, is blown up by Union engineers, and the Battle of the Crater ensues. Despite catching the Confederate line off guard, the Union attack is a fiasco, resulting in almost 4000 Union casualties.

AUGUST 5

The Battle of Mobile Bay, Alabama, is won by Admiral Farragut of the Union. Declaring, "Damn the torpedoes! Full speed ahead!" the admiral gains a valuable Confederate port.

SEPTEMBER 2

After a four-week siege, General Sherman captures Atlanta, announcing in a telegram, "So Atlanta is ours, and fairly won."

NOVEMBER 8

In an electoral landslide, Abraham Lincoln defeats General McClellan to win a second term as president of the United States. McClellan resigns his army commission.

NOVEMBER 16

Abandoning their supply train and living off the land, General Sherman's forces begin their march through Georgia to the sea.

NOVEMBER 30

Confederate general John Bell Hood leads the Battle of Franklin, Tennessee. Consisting of a full-scale assault across open fields against Union entrenchments, the battle results in heavy losses for the South, including the death of six Confederate generals.

DECEMBER 15–16

The Battle of Nashville, Tennessee. In a devastating defeat for the Confederacy, the Army of Tennessee is left incapable of active operations. Only General Lee's Army of Northern Virginia stands in the way of outright Union victory.

DECEMBER 21

Savannah, Georgia, falls to the forces of General Sherman, who gives the city to Lincoln as a Christmas present.

1865

JANUARY 31

The Thirteenth Amendment is passed by the House of Representatives, abolishing slavery.

FEBRUARY 17

Columbia, South Carolina, is destroyed by fire, possibly started by General Sherman's troops, or perhaps by retreating Confederates.

MARCH 4

Lincoln delivers his second inaugural address. Proclaiming, "With malice toward none, with charity for all," the president looks to the future with his vision of peace.

APRIL 1

The Battle of Five Forks, Virginia. Large numbers of Confederate troops fighting under Major General George E. Pickett are taken prisoner, further isolating General Lee's army.

APRIL 2

The Union Army breaks through at Petersburg, Virginia, and enters the Confederate capital at Richmond. Jefferson Davis and his cabinet flee south, deeper into the Confederacy, as Richmond burns.

APRIL 6

Union forces win the Battle of Sailor's Creek, Virginia, cutting off General Lee's retreat.

APRIL 9

Following the Union victory at Sailor's Creek, General Lee surrenders his Army of Northern Virginia to General Grant at Appomattox Court House, Virginia.

APRIL 14

Stage actor John Wilkes Booth shoots Abraham Lincoln at Ford's Theater in Washington, D.C. The president dies the next morning.

APRIL 26

General Johnston surrenders his 30,000-strong Army of Tennessee to General Sherman in North Carolina. Elsewhere, John Wilkes Booth

is shot in a tobacco barn in Virginia and dies a few hours later.

APRIL 27

More than 1200 passengers aboard the *Sultana*, a steam-powered riverboat, are killed when the boilers burst. Most of the dead are Union soldiers recently released from Confederate prisoner-of-war camps.

MAY 10

Jefferson Davis is captured near Irwinville, Georgia.

JUNE 2

Confederate general E. Kirby Smith, commander of the Trans-Mississippi Department, accepts the terms of his surrender, formally ending Confederate resistance.

JUNE 30

All eight suspects charged with conspiring to assassinate President Lincoln are found guilty. Four are sentenced to death, and, on July 7, are hanged at the Old Arsenal Penitentiary in Washington, D.C.

BATTLEFIELDS AND ORGANIZATIONS

CIVIL WAR BATTLEFIELDS AND SITES PHOTOGRAPHED

Cedar Creek Battlefield, Middletown, Virginia
www.cedarcreekbattlefield.org

Drum Barracks Civil War Museum, Wilmington, California
www.drumbarracks.org

Gettysburg National Military Park, Pennsylvania
www.nps.gov/gett

McDowell Battlefield, Virginia
www.shenandoahatwar.org

Manassas National Battlefield Park, Virginia
www.nps.gov/mana

New Market Battlefield State Historical Park, Virginia
www2.vmi.edu/museum/nm/index.html

Perryville Battlefield, Kentucky
www.perryvillebattlefield.org

Raymond Battlefield, Mississippi
www.battleofraymond.org

Wilson's Creek National Battlefield Foundation, Springfield, Missouri
www.wilsonscreek.com

ADDITIONAL SOURCES OF INFORMATION ON CIVIL WAR BATTLEFIELDS

Civil War Trust
www.civilwar.org

National Park Service Sesquicentennial Commemoration
www.nps.gov/civilwar150

REENACTMENT ORGANIZATIONS

UNITED STATES

Blue-Gray Alliance
www.150thcivilwarevents.com

Civil War Alliance
www.civilwaralliance.com

Cleburne's Division of Reenactors
www.cleburnes-division.com

First Federal Division
www.firstfederaldivision.com

Historical Citizens Association
www.historicalcitizens.org

The Southern Division
www.southerndivision.org

Western Federal Blues
www.westernfederalblues.org

FRANCE

Club Confédéré et Fédéral de France
www.ccffcw.xooit.fr

GERMANY

Union and Confederate Reenactors International
www.ucr-ev.de

UNITED KINGDOM

American Civil War Society (UK)
www.acws.co.uk

Lazy Jacks Mess
www.lazyjackmess.com

Southern Skirmish Association
www.soskan.co.uk

INDEX

ACKNOWLEDGMENTS

We are grateful to a number of people and organizations whose help made this book possible.

Enormous thanks go to Hugh Merrell and Merrell Publishers for believing in this project and our work. Thanks also go to James Lighthizer, president of the Civil War Trust, who works tirelessly to preserve Civil War battlefields and, by extension, American history.

We appreciate the help of Robert Lee Hodge; Chris Anders; Chad Greene; Bob Denton and the Thirty-Seventh Virginia, Company K, of Pridgeon's Shenandoah Legion; the American Civil War Society (UK); Mar'Ellen Felin and the Wilson's Creek National Battlefield Foundation; Nikki Brown and Prince William County, Virginia; the Friends of Raymond, Mississippi; the First Texas Volunteer Infantry; Ed Mann; Janet Whaley; Ivan Rose; Clovis Davis; Will Dunniway; Wayne Pierce; Scott Waldeck at House of Hardwood in Los Angeles, California; and Gonzalo Santiago.

Special thanks go to Terry Handy; our agent, Neil Salkind; Susan Ogle, director of the Drum Barracks Civil War Museum in Wilmington, California; Julie and Brandon Booth; Paula and Greg Agar; and our families and friends.

Finally, to the reenactors who dedicate themselves to keeping alive the sacrifices that soldiers and civilians made during the Civil War, thank you for allowing us to be a part of your world.

PICTURE CREDITS

All photographs are by Mark Elson, with the exception of the following images by Mathew Brady:

PAGE 12 (LEFT)
Library of Congress, Prints and Photographs Division (LC-DIG-cwpb-01450 DLC)

PAGE 14 (RIGHT)
Library of Congress, Prints and Photographs Division (LC-B8184-10368 DLC)

Digital scans of Mark Elson's photographs were produced by Don Weinstein, master printer, in Los Angeles, California.

First published in 2012 by Merrell Publishers, London and New York

Merrell Publishers Limited
81 Southwark Street
London SE1 0HX

merrellpublishers.com

A catalog record for this book is available from the Library
of Congress.

British Library Cataloguing-in-Publication Data:
Elson, Mark.
Battlefields of honor : American Civil War reenactors.
1. United States—History—Civil War, 1861–1865—Pictorial works.
2. Historical reenactments—United States—Pictorial works.
I. Title II. Stein, Jeannine.
973.7'0222-dc23

ISBN 978-1-8589-4578-1

Produced by Merrell Publishers Limited
Designed by Nicola Bailey
Project-managed by Mark Ralph
Indexed by Hilary Bird

Printed and bound in China

JACKET, FRONT (FROM TOP)
See pages 128 (top) and 129.

JACKET, BACK (FROM TOP)
See pages 114–15 and 75.

FRONT FLAP
See page 89 (right).

PAGES 2–3
See page 116 (bottom).

PAGE 4
Reenactors from a Texas regiment prepare to go on a march
in Southern California.
Wet-plate photograph

PAGE 176
A Union drummer at the site of the Battle of Raymond in
Mississippi hears the sound of distant fighting.

The stanza of verse on page 176 is taken from 'The Blue and
the Gray' (1867) by Francis Miles Finch (1827–1907). For the
full text of the poem, see *The Blue and the Gray and Other Verses*
(Henry Holt & Co., 1909).

No more shall the war cry sever,
    Or the winding rivers be red;
They banish our anger forever
    When they laurel the graves of our dead!
Under the sod and the dew,
    Waiting the judgment-day,
Love and tears for the Blue,
    Tears and love for the Gray.